MW00436371

Printed in the United States of America

First Printing 2020

ISBN: 978-0-9965556-9-2

Firefly Grace Publishing
Burlington, VT 05403
www.EmilyRLong.com

Pregnancy After Loss Support
Bloomington, MN 55437
www.pregnancyafterlosssupport.org

Pregnancy After Loss Support:
Love Letters to Moms Pregnant After Loss

Gratitude and Dedication

Emily's Dedication

With immense gratitude to Dr. Jennie Lowell, for helping me bring to a close and find peace with my journey of pregnancy and motherhood.
A medical provider who listens, respects, and honors a grieving mother's needs is an invaluable gift.

Lindsey's Dedication

This book is dedicated to every mother who has ever lost a baby.
May you know that you are not alone as you navigate both hope and fear while nurturing your grief during your pregnancy that follows a loss.

Other Available Books by Emily Long

Invisible Mothers: When Love Doesn't Die

You Are Not Alone: Love Letters from Loss Mom to Loss Mom

From Father to Father: Letters from Loss Dad to Loss Dad

Life Without the Baby Journal: Redefining Life, Motherhood and Self After Loss

From Mother to Mother: On the Loss of a Child

Fathers Speak: On the Death of a Child

PALS

Pregnancy After Loss Support

choosing hope over fear while nurturing grief

Pregnancy After Loss Support (PALS) is a 501(c) (3) non-profit organization and community support resource for women experiencing the confusing and conflicting emotions of grief mixed with joy during the journey through pregnancy after loss. PALS seeks to help expectant mothers celebrate their current pregnancy by choosing hope over fear while still nurturing and honoring the grief over the loss of their deceased child.

PALS services include an online magazine, online peer-moderated support groups, local meet-ups, outreach and education through speaking and tabling at professional conferences, resource listings for families and healthcare providers, and a newsletter.

- Website: https://pregnancyafterlosssupport. com/
- Facebook: https://www.facebook.com/ pregnancyafterlosssupport/
- Twitter: @PALS_Support
- Instagram: @pregnancyafterlosssupport

To the One Holding Both Hope and Fear,

I wish I could give you a guarantee of a living baby. I wish I could return the innocent hope and excitement of the person who had not yet experienced the death of their baby. I wish I could give you a pregnancy full of untainted joy and excitement and anticipation.

Unfortunately, I cannot.

If you were here with me in person, I'd offer you a comfy chair and a cup of hot chocolate (extra marshmallows).

Then I would give you my ears, to hear and hold all your hopes and fears and that wretched fear of hope.

I'd lend you my shoulders when you needed to cry.

When you needed to laugh, I'd offers you silly stories and cheesy jokes until that fist of fear in your chest loosened just the slightest bit.

I'd sit in the quiet with you when you needed to escape into sleep.

I'd talk with you about the baby(ies) that couldn't stay and the dreams you held for them.

I'd listen to your hopes and fears for this new life growing inside you now.

When fear takes over, I'd hold that space and light of hope and joy and anticipation for you until you can find them again.

Unfortunately, I can't do those things either.

What I can do is let you know that you are not alone. While I can't hold your hand or hug you tight, I can offer the love in this book. I can give you words and love from others like you who have held both hope and fear.

I can give you these words on these pages, something to reach for when things feel dark, when fear feels overwhelming, and when you need to know you are not the only one.

You are not alone.
You are not alone.
You are not alone.

With so much love, a friend, willing to sit in the messiness of the grief, the uncertainty, the hope and the fear with you,

Emily Long

Mama to Grace & Lily
Website: www.emilyrlong.com
Instagram: @long.emily
Facebook: www.facebook.com/invisiblemothers

"*You are not alone.*
You are not alone.
You are not alone."

Dear Courageous Mama,

I am you. Right now I am currently 31 weeks pregnant with my baby after the loss of my first, and only child, at 40 weeks pregnant with my beautiful daughter. I know you, because I am you. I may not have all the same thoughts or the same experiences as you, but I can say I know. I know this is hard because it's hard for me. It's the most difficult thing I have ever done after giving birth to and burying my stillborn baby girl.

I'm sorry to say that I don't have any advice, as I'm not on the other side. I am in the thick of it just like you and even if I was holding my current baby safely in my arms alive, I'm still not sure I would know the right words to say. What I can share with you are my true feelings and, honestly, I'm really scared right now. The truth is that every morning for the past five weeks I wake up terrified that my baby has died in the previous hours that I have slept, like my one before her did. My heart pounds and my mind races with morbid thoughts of once again delivering a dead child until all of the sudden a familiar poke tickles my hand as I am reassured my baby is still alive inside me with the somersault I feel her completing within.

You see, in that same moment, the one that was filled with terror before, is where gratitude also finds me and fills my soul with peace and an overwhelming sense of appreciation that I have been granted one more day, another chance, at bringing a living soul into this world. To say the least, it's confusing; to wake to these kinds of emotions each day and hoping to relive them tomorrow because that would mean that my one wish is still true. That my baby will be born breathing and healthy and most importantly – ALIVE.

Maybe this letter doesn't sound reassuring, but it is honest and to continue on this note of truth I would like to tell you that I do, oh how I do, try and try so hard to find joy in this pregnancy. Each day I battle back anxiety, depression, anger, frustration, sadness, grief, and PTSD symptoms in an effort to choose joy over fear. Sometimes I win. But other days fear finds me again, usually in the moments when I begin to let my guard down and envision a life with a smiling, giggling, crying, breathing, living baby girl. Here is where the ugliness of fear rears its head, saying "Remember, this pregnancy is only a trick, just like your last, you are not worthy of such a little blessing." But, I will not believe this liar known as fear and I fight back! I feel the fear, welcome him and all of his deceptions, and choose joy anyway!!! Even though it's hard as hell to do, I yell back in fear's face and say, "TODAY I CHOOSE JOY!"

In doing this I find a moment of peace that settles into my tired body and soul. Then I look down at my round stomach and stroke my belly all the while praying to a God I don't believe in, and a Universe that I no longer trust, to give me the strength to make it through this journey and remember to just take each day as a gift. If I have learned anything over the past 14 months, it's that I only get this day. This gift. This moment. I only get now and in that now I want it to be filled with happiness, not fear. I want my baby girl to know love, not dread. And each day that is what I will give her by choosing joy. It's not easy, like I said, It's one of the hardest things I've ever had to do.

But I'm doing it. Just like you. WE are doing it. Just by having the courage to try again we are choosing joy. Just by waking up each morning and facing what obstacles and anxieties pregnancy throws at us we are choosing joy. Just by being brave enough to be pregnant again we are choosing joy. Remember, we, both you and I, are courageous warriors who have stared down the face of fear and said, "I don't choose you. I choose joy instead!" just by being here, wherever we are on this road of pregnancy after loss, just by saying yes to hopes of other chances and choosing joy, we have won.

Today, we have won.

Love,

Lindsey Henke

Fellow PAL Mom & Courageous PAL Warrior
Mom to Nora, Zoe & Liev
LindseyMHenke.com

out of your mouth each time a passerby congratulates you or responds to your growing belly or inquires about your plans. "If this baby lives," you say. "Maybe we'll paint the nursery blue, but first let's see if we get to bring this one home."

You are fighting a battle indeed. And the memory of defeat is never far from your mind. You remember being stomped by the crushing weight of your baby's death. You remember blood and pain and trauma. You remember crawling through the trenches of grief alone. And you wonder if you are in for it again.

It's a long and trying battle. But you are a warrior.

You fell to your knees after saying goodbye to a baby who suddenly vanished. You thought you'd been promised life only to be handed death. But you refused to stay down. Slowly, you stood back up, reclaiming your strength and chose to try again, taking another chance at life.

In the midst of a battle between belief and doubt, you choose to believe that this time will be different. When doubt says you're a fool, you choose to believe that your baby is worth fighting for.

In the midst of a battle between hope and hopelessness, you choose to hope that your baby will come home with you. You recall being left in the most hopeless of situations as you once said goodbye, but you cling to the hope that this time you'll get to say hello.

In the midst of a battle between courage and fear,

you choose courage. Even though it's scary, you are willing to take a chance on life, on love. And you allow courage to navigate this journey of unknowns.

In the midst of a battle between life and death, you cherish life, for you are uncertain how long it will last. When death overshadows your pregnancy, you cling to the life growing within. And you imagine its potential.

Each day as you rise out of bed, you choose to fight. Each day as you muddle through the long hours, you choose to fight.
Each night when you are unsure of what tomorrow brings, you choose to fight.

Because you are a warrior. And you are a mother. And you were made to fight for your baby, for life.

Hold tight, mama. Even when your entire being tells you that pregnancy loss is the end, keep fighting to believe that pregnancy after loss might just be the beginning. You are a warrior. And while the battle isn't over, you'll keep fighting for the life that has just begun.

Jenny Albers

Mom to Baby A and Micah
Facebook & Instagram @abeautifullyburdenedlife
abeautifullyburdenedlife.com

"Each day as you rise out of bed, you choose to fight.
Each day as you muddle through the long hours, you
choose to fight.
Each night when you are unsure of what tomorrow brings,
you choose to fight.

Because you are a warrior. And you are a mother. And
you were made to fight for your baby, for life."

You Brave and Beautiful Soul,

I want to tell you, Congratulations.

This might be a word that you feel doesn't belong to you, but let me tell you, it does.

Congratulations on getting pregnant. That is no small feat for some, especially with the havoc grief can wreak on your hormones. Congratulations for having the tenacity to try again. Here you are - on the path you were so cruelly and unfairly thrust off of in the past - and you're doing it. You're doing it! Not to mention, you've somehow managed to open this book to find some support, so good for you. Pregnancy after loss is beyond challenging, and sometimes we have to disconnect in the name of self-preservation. But I think if you have picked up this book, you have already taken a really incredible step towards managing to engage in some self-care during this pregnancy. For that, you should be applauded. So bravo!

So many people in our lives can't begin to understand the depth of anxiety, stress, and fear that comes along with pregnancy after loss. Managing the response to trauma is a full-time job in itself, never mind finding the courage to take care of this new baby by taking care of yourself.

I was so angry at my body for so long. Our first child, Mathilda died shortly before she was born at 40 weeks. Then, cruelly, we struggled with infertility. It was salt in the wound that our only baby died and then we weren't sure if we'd be able to conceive again. After infertility treatment we were able to get pregnant, which was incredible, but it was so hard to shift my way of thinking. I now had to try and take care of this body that had let me down. This body I had been basically ignoring until then. We managed to go on to have a living child and I was so proud of myself - I got through it and we came out the other side with a beautiful baby girl. I could breathe again. Then, when she was just 8 days old, we were rushed to Boston Children's Hospital because of an undiagnosed critical coarctation of her aorta that required life-saving emergency surgery. Thankfully she survived and is now thriving, but in those moments I couldn't help but blame myself, my body.

When we decided that we would regret not trying to give her a living sibling and that we were willing to try again - it was another struggle with continued infertility. I had to take care of myself, almost in spite of myself. I had to just force myself to believe that I could have a healthy living baby - one that could be born alive and not need a life-saving surgery to survive. It was one of the hardest things I've ever done. I also tried to enjoy what I could of that third pregnancy because I knew I would never want to do it again. Enjoy is not the right word - maybe find moments of being truly present? Savor some things so that I could remember the details when (and at the time 'if') my child one day asked me about it.

I was someone who had to constantly use precursors like 'hopefully' and 'if' instead of 'when.' Once I stopped apologizing for it and embraced the fact that I needed these precursors, I felt a little better. That is what I needed to take care of myself. I didn't want to jinx anything (as if that's possible). And it's okay if you can't go all-in on the possibility of a living baby being placed in your aching arms - but if you are able to believe it, even just for some of the time, don't guilt yourself for it. It's all hard enough.

I guess what I'm trying to say is, give yourself permission to handle this pregnancy in whatever way you need to. However feels best to think about (or not think about) this sweet baby that you so desperately want is truly up to you. Don't let anyone else tell you how you should feel; because you are the only person who can know what it is to take this leap of faith and trust your body again, a body that you may feel betrayed you in the past. I wish I could tell you that everything will be okay and that lightning never strikes twice, or some other platitude that I am sure has been thrown your way. Unfortunately, we all know that isn't true and no one can guarantee anything in this life - we loss parents know that better than anyone.

What I can say is that you're doing it! I also want to remind you that there is room for all of your emotions - you can feel joy and anticipation while experiencing deep fear and dread. We are complicated creatures, capable of feeling all of these things - often at the same time - so allow these feelings to come. I have found that acknowledging them and giving them some space will serve you far better than trying to ignore them or feel guilty for having them.

Life will always be bittersweet. Their absence is relentless. I can say that you will get better at carrying that weight. I am sure you are better at it now than you were the day after your life changed forever. The same is true of having a living child. You will figure out how to negotiate all the milestones, the lost sibling experiences, not being able to parent all of your children together in the same physical space - you will figure out what works best for you and it will continue to change and grow as you and your beautiful family do.

I am proud of you. You are doing it. I am quietly in your corner rooting for you - along with all of the other bereaved parents. On days where you feel like it's all too heavy, remember that we are here. Feel our vibrations of love and well wishes in the air around you. Breathe it in and let the courage inside of you grown just a little bit stronger. Let that love bloom inside of your heart and take it one moment at a time. You're doing it!

In love and solidarity,

Darcie

Mathilda (born still March 4th, 2016), Winslow, and Hugo's Mama
https://lostlullabies.weebly.com/

"I am proud of you. You are doing it. I am quietly in your corner rooting for you - along with all of the other bereaved parents. On days where you feel like it's all too heavy, remember that we are here."

Dear Mama Who Feels Like She's Failing,

I know how much you long to have a child. And not just any child, but the child you had before, the child you are pregnant with now, and the child who is still to come. I know what it feels like to do All. The. Things. to make sure your child is safe and healthy, to do your very best to bring them to your arms, and for the process to go epically wrong. Then to feel that you are failing at this journey to family.

I know what it feels like to get that positive pregnancy test, look at the longing in your husband's eyes, and clam up wondering if your body is going to do what it needs to do. I've been in those heart-sinking moments where you realize the miscarriage began and you have to tell your partner, "not this time." And the unwanted, unearned guilt that creeps up despite your best efforts. The guilt that says you alone were responsible for this little life, and your best was not enough. And then the guilt that not only will your partner now not have this child, but he will also need to support you through your grief.

It's a stupid guilt, a wrong guilt, a guilt made up of nothing but lies. And yet, you feel it all the same.

Oh mama. I know what it is to feel like you've let everyone down — even when you haven't.
I know what it feels like to think you're handling this journey all wrong. Handling all the emotions, all the losses, all the trying in between. I know what it's like to feel like you're failing medical tests when they come back without an answer. To feel like you're so caught up in what wasn't, you're missing everything that is.

You begin judging not just your efforts to have a baby, but the all-encompassing desire to have that baby.

I know what it's like to have a living child want a sibling so badly she asked for a different house. Because the house was surely the problem, right? Not the fact that her mama couldn't carry her babies to term. My daughter's imploring innocence gutted me. Oh how badly I longed to give her the sister that she was supposed to have. Oh how much I longed to see her watching my belly swell, meet her newborn sibling, and watch as their relationship grew over the years. Her ache matched my own, but it was an ache I literally could not fill. I could be the right mama to her in a million ways — but in that one way, I felt as though I would never be enough.

I know what it's like to finally see that positive pregnancy test, and then instantly be consumed by fear that your body would fail your baby, fail you, and fail your family. And as the pregnancy continues, and your baby goes from peppercorn to acorn to carrot to watermelon, the pressure grows. I know what it's like to worry you aren't properly thankful for this baby as you're consumed with anxiety. Could it be possible to fail at a successful pregnancy?

And the question I faced, and face every single day, is how can I move forward when I'm so afraid of letting everyone down? When I feel as though I HAVE let everyone down?

I'm writing this letter to you, dear mama, but you'll see I'm also writing it to me. Because we both have felt the condemnation, the crazy-making questions, the burden of responsibility which is not ours to bear.

And I'm here to tell you that not only are you not alone in all of this. (Because YOU ARE NOT ALONE. Please hear me on this.) But you and I can also be free from all this pressure we feel to be enough.

Did you know we don't have to shoulder the responsibility to provide a sibling for our other children, a daughter or son for our partner, or a grandchild for our parents? Reproduction is not a right, as much as I wish it were. And it's not a competition where if we just practice hard enough, put in enough effort, we'll come home with the reward.

We live in a broken world, and all the rules are off the table when it comes to having babies. Sometimes moms caught in addiction, parents who are abusive, teenagers struggling with stability seem to have an uncanny ability to pop out babies. And sometimes women who have done every single thing according to the rules are left without a baby in their arms. It is crazy-making, I know. But there is a gift in this for us if we can just see it.

Just as we don't deserve a child, we don't un-deserve one either.

Do you hear me on this? It means that you have not failed.

When you feel that pit in your stomach that says you are not enough, I'm here and God's here to tell you, YES. YOU ARE ENOUGH.

When you are facing a pregnancy riddled with anxiety, and you can't help but question if you're doing it all wrong, I'm here and God's here to say, MAMA. YOU GOT THIS. JUST TAKE IT MOMENT BY MOMENT.

When you look around and see the disappointment around you at your loss, and you feel like their feelings are on you, I'm here and God's here to say, MAMA, THIS IS NOT YOUR BURDEN TO BEAR. Lay it down, sweet one. Lay it down.

When your sweet rainbow is in your arms, and you wonder if the joy you hold betrays the sorrow of your lost baby, I'm here and God's here to say, LOVE CANNOT BE SUBTRACTED. YOUR LOVE IS BIG ENOUGH FOR THEM BOTH.

When you know you can't take one more loss, and you need to stop your journey to pregnancy, I'm here and God's here to say, MAMA, YOU ARE THE MOST COURAGEOUS OF THEM ALL.

And when you think for one hot minute that you are the only one who's ever felt like they are failing on this journey, I'm here and God's here to say, YOU ARE NOT ALONE. AND YOU ARE LOVED THROUGH IT ALL.

Dear mama who feels like you're failing . . .

You are enough, just as you are.

All my love and admiration,

Rachel Lewis

Proud mama to Olivia Joy and the Lewis babies.
thelewisnote.com
facebook.com/TheLewisNote
facebook.com/groups/bravemamas
instagram.com/rachel.thelewisnote

"You are enough, just as you are."

Dear Mama Afraid to Hope,

It can be hard to believe this is real. You may feel like you will never get to the end of this pregnancy. 40 weeks can feel like 40 years in a pregnancy after loss. You may not believe that you will bring a living baby home.

Are you feeling scared? Are you numbing yourself to emotions? Are you bracing yourself for another heartbreak at every appointment? Do you feel like experiencing any joy or expressing any hope at all will result in that being immediately stolen from you... again?

Is it hard to be hopeful?

Oh sweet mama, I know how that is. When I was pregnant again after losing my first child at 20 weeks, I vowed to enjoy every moment. Savor every bout of nausea, every flare of heartburn, every bit of discomfort - be it from my body changing or from medical procedures necessary to keep us safe. I felt guilty because I took for granted time spent with my first baby, I wasn't going to do that the second time around. I was going to cherish every second.

But then my cervix started shortening, and we worried about an incompetent cervix surfacing again. Then I started having contractions at 24 weeks and subsequently was put on bed rest until delivery or 36 weeks, whichever came first. We were meeting with doctors about preterm delivery and what it would be like to have a preemie. We discussed survival rates at 28 weeks versus 32 weeks versus 36 weeks. We thought in terms of "if" rather than "when."

I stopped believing he would be born alive. I started losing hope that I would bring my baby home.

So what saved me during this anxious time? A few things. My therapist was there to remind me feel whatever I was feeling. But also that if I felt excited about this baby, it would not hurt more if I lost this baby. Refraining from joy would not mitigate the pain if something happened again.

I had to force myself to find 10 minutes a day to find joy. There was a conscious effort on my part to celebrate something – anything – while pregnant.

I bought myself a small a bunny holding a star reading "HOPE" that I kept by my bed. Bunnies remind me of my first baby and this felt like a sign from her that it was not only okay that I was pregnant again, but also that she was hopeful for me too. It was a small daily reminder for me to not give up.

But what helped me most of all was other PAL mamas. Knowing and confiding in other moms who had travelled this path before me and knew exactly what I was feeling helped immensely. These moms would go on to snuggle their newborns who were born alive and healthy. They were real life examples that dreams do come true.

So when you feel all hope is gone, try some of these things. Force yourself to focus on the joy you feel for this baby, even if for only 10 minutes a day. Seek out other moms who are experiencing pregnancy after loss. Find a hopeful mantra or sign to place somewhere you'll see it every day.

> "If your wings are broken, borrow mine so yours can open too." – Rachel Platten

Also, remind yourself of all the courageous mamas who came before you. Remember our journeys. Remember our rainbow babies who are thriving today. We made it through this, and you will too.

And if it is all still too much to bear, let us hold onto hope for you. Let us remind you there's a light at the end of the tunnel. I know all too well that it can be so hard to feel hopeful after such devastating loss, but I know there's joy after all of this.

So, let us carry you through the fear to joy and the hope of the rainbow after the storm.

With love,

Rebecca Markert

Mom of Lilith Ann (Lily), Dexter, Audrey, Owen and Jaxon

"And if it is all still too much to bear, let us hold onto hope for you. Let us remind you there's a light at the end of the tunnel. I know all too well that it can be so hard to feel hopeful after such devastating loss, but I know there's joy after all of this."

Dear Mama,

It is okay to be scared.

Pregnancy after loss is scary. Scarier than I ever imagined it would be.

I knew that I would be nervous and anxious and sad, but I never imagined being so scared.

I was scared to go to my midwife appointments.
I was scared to go to ultrasounds.
I was scared to announce my pregnancy.
I was scared to have a baby shower.

I was scared for 9 months and it was exhausting. I wanted more than anything to be excited and hopeful, but there was a looming doubt of not wanting to get my hopes up that never fully went away.

I wish there was a phrase or quote I could tell you that would take the fear away, but if you are like me there was nothing anyone could say to ease my fear. So rather than try to take your fear away I want to acknowledge your fear, and tell you it is okay.

You are scared because of how much you love. How much you love the baby who isn't with you earth side. How much you love the baby within you now. How much you love being a mom. You are scared because you love them all so much and it is okay.

I am blessed to have my rainbow baby beside me at this very moment, and while I can say that those

9 months were long and scary and filled with more anxiety and tears than I ever thought possible to cry, I can also say it was worth it.

So please remember Mama, you are strong and courageous and being scared doesn't change that. You got this.

With love,

Meg Kant

Zennon, Gibson, and Miller

"You are scared because of how much you love. How much you love the baby who isn't with you earth side. How much you love the baby within you now. How much you love being a mom. You are scared because you love them all so much and it is okay."

Dear Courageous Mama...Pregnant with your Last Child after a Loss,

Not that long ago, I was you. I was standing where you are standing right now. I was pregnant with my rainbow baby, my LAST baby.

I will not lie. As happy as I was, I was terrified too. Pregnancy after loss is not an easy path to tread. It was not the journey I wanted for me. It's not a journey any of us would choose, but I want you to hear these words, sweet mama. You can do this! Yes, it's going to be the one of the hardest things you've ever done. Yes, it's going to be scary at times, but I promise you it will also be full of so much hope, beauty, and love that sometimes your heart will feel like it's going to explode with joy.

As emotional as a PAL pregnancy is, knowing that it's your last pregnancy makes it more bittersweet – if such a thing is possible. Embrace all of those feelings, courageous mama. Every single one. They are yours. You have earned them, especially the happy ones.

Sweet mama, I know that ever since you found out you were pregnant and knew THIS was the final time, it seems like the days are creeping slowly by. Your body has betrayed you before, and you are afraid it will again. You are looking forward to the moment when your baby will finally be here, alive, safe, and where you never have to take your eyes off of him (or her) again.

It seems like that day will never come, especially on those anxious days when you worry more than usual.

Maybe you're not quite sure if your baby is moving as much as he usually does, so you go in to see your OB for one extra monitoring. It's reassuring to hear that strong, fast fetal heartbeat and the swooshes (and feel the kicks) while your son tries to kick to monitor off because it's too restraining around your belly. Maybe it's the weekend and you can't get those contractions to stop, even after guzzling water and lying on your side, so you head to labor and delivery again. Whatever the reason for calling your OB office and asking to speak with the nurse or calling the on-call doctor and waking her up at 1 am., you don't feel silly at all because they know you've already lost a baby and that you are higher risk this time. They also know that this is your last baby, so you're all kinds of emotional and determined to make sure that everything goes as OK as it possibly can.

Yes, courageous mama, when you first learn that you are pregnant with your final child after a loss, it seems like you are pregnant forever, or at least as long as an elephant gestates. It's scary to think about how much can go wrong in the days between conception and delivery, and Google is not your friend when you are worried about every single new symptom you are experiencing.

Not long ago, I was you. I was standing where you are standing. Happy, terrified, and ready to embrace my last baby. But now that my rainbow is here, I want to tell you, as scary as my PAL pregnancy was, I miss it too. It went by much quicker than I realized it would.

I miss the first time I felt him move...and how happy it made me feel because I KNEW he was really there. I miss the way his brother and sister squealed in delight the first time they felt him kick…and how surprised they were that someone so tiny could be so strong. I miss the way he got hiccups every single day…and how I could set my phone on my belly and watch it dance. My family got a big laugh out of that one too. I miss the way his daddy would put his mouth against my belly and chant "1, 2, 3, 4! I love the Marine Corps!" That would really make him kick hard. I even kind of miss the yucky stuff like the morning sickness and the achy back and waddling around. I'd do it all over again.

I have a lot of pictures and I wrote a lot about my pregnancy, but some of my favorite memories are just that – memories. Snapshots and sound bytes that only exist in my head. I'll never forget the first time I heard my last baby cry or the way I cried too, knowing he was finally here – alive and safe. I'll never forget the first time I saw his daddy hold him or how gentle he was picking him up that first time. I'll never forget the first time the nurse handed him to me or how I kissed him and whispered, "Hello, my love. I'm your mommy, and I love you." I never wanted to let him go.

It's OK to be scared, mama. It's ok to anxiously await your baby's arrival, but take a moment to enjoy to little things. Looking back, those little things are the big things. Embrace this pregnancy as fully as you feel comfortable embracing it. As much as you are looking forward to holding your precious baby in your arms, one day you're going to miss the closeness you're sharing together right now.

Take a picture. Make a memory. Breathe! Enjoy THIS moment.

Love,

Tara Bennet

Mom to Cole, Lara, Jesse and Zuri
Thisoldladyhadababy.blogspot.com

"As emotional as a PAL pregnancy is, knowing that it's your last pregnancy makes it more bittersweet – if such a thing is possible. Embrace all of those feelings, courageous mama. Every single one. They are yours. You have earned them, especially the happy ones."

Dear Mama Who Feels Confused,

I want you to know it's OK. No, it is not OK that you lost your baby(ies). That will never be OK. What is OK is to feel whatever you're feeling. Scared. Hopeful. Sad. Exhausted. Determined. Angry. Detached. Confused. Excited. The list of emotions is endless, and often cycled through within moments each day. It's OK to feel the feelings—good and bad. Acknowledging these emotions can help you understand and process what you're going through.

It's OK to ask for help.

Whether it is from your partner, family or friends, clergy, doctor, therapist, or PAL Support Group, there's no shame in recognizing you need help to get you through this pregnancy. You've been through a lot. Be gentle with yourself and find the support you need to ease this process.

It's OK to be scared.

Of course you're going to be scared, your history has shown you what could happen. While most "regular" women can look at various pregnancy points gleefully down the road, we PAL Moms have to focus on this. very. moment. Being scared is normal, and all the more reason to have a good support system set up. Trying to stay present, while focusing on the fact that this was a different pregnancy helped me...sometimes.

It's OK to be happy and sad at the same time.

PAL brings on just about every oxymoron of emotions. Of course you're grateful for this new life growing inside of you. You're hopeful about the little one's life ahead. Your giddy with the first kick and every movement afterwards. And at the same time, each of these moments may remind you of what you didn't/ won't have with your previous child(ren). It's OK to enjoy those happy moments while honoring the lost ones.

It's OK to bond. It's OK to feel detached.

I wanted nothing more than to embrace my pregnancy, and there were times where I was fully able to. After wanting to be surprised in our earlier pregnancies, we found out the sex as early as possible, since it turned out, that the surprise would be if the baby was born healthy and breathing. I'd talk to J, rub my belly and try to visualize a positive outcome. I also found myself holding my breath, stepping back and not allowing myself to think about the future. It's OK to bond, detach or fluctuate between the two.

It's OK to hide. It's OK to shout it from the rooftops.

Maybe you, like me, don't want to deal with people's looks and comments. Maybe you want everyone to know to be able to support and provide you with their positive energy. There is no right answer here. What there is, is doing what's right for you. Just remember, this is about what you (and your partner) want, not what anyone else wants, or what you think they want.

It's OK to consider adoption (or another path to family). It's OK if you're done trying to conceive and carry on your own.

You might think that considering adoption after loss may make you less of a Mom. I'm here to tell you, a Mom is a Mom. I now have two beautiful boys at home: one arrived via adoption, and one I was able to carry to term, and deliver healthy and breathing. And you know what? They're both my sons. No matter what decision you make to build your family, you're still going to be the one to get up in the middle of the night to feed your baby. You're still going to be the one they run to when they get hurt. You're the one they're going to call Mom. It may not be the way you envisioned becoming a family, but you are, in fact, a family.

It's OK.
This list could go on and on. What's important to remember is that pretty much anything you're feeling or doing is OK. What's not OK is if these feelings or actions are harmful—physically or mentally—to you or your baby. You don't have to do this alone. They say it takes a village to raise a child, and for us PAL moms, it takes a village to get through another pregnancy.

Pregnancy after loss, like life after loss is an ever-changing path. And while each of us walks a similar path, none of our experiences are exactly alike. Each of our shared voices remind us that we're not alone.

You're not alone. We're here.

From one courageous and determined loss Mom to another, just remember, it's OK.

Love,

Erin Kuhn-Krueger

Mom to Baby Krueger, Sarah Hana and Benjamin
Samuel, and the 4 we never met
Willcarryon.wordpress.com
Facebook & Twitter @ErinKuhnKrueger

"PAL brings on just about every oxymoron of emotions. Of course you're grateful for this new life growing inside of you. You're hopeful about the little one's life ahead. Your giddy with the first kick and every movement afterwards. And at the same time, each of these moments may remind you of what you didn't/won't have with your previous child(ren). It's OK to enjoy those happy moments while honoring the lost ones."

Dear Mama,

It's harder to know how now, isn't it? We all begin
innocently enough. We pee on a stick. We jump up and
down. We kiss our partners. We think, there, we've
done it; we're having a baby.

Then, you don't.

Then, maybe, you don't again.

Then, maybe, you do.

Maybe, that first time, you also had three baby
showers, "too soon" as it would turn out, and found
yourself with a closet full of clothes and toys and bibs
and bottles. Maybe you tell yourself you should donate
it all, let everything be used. Maybe you marvel at how
difficult it would be to give away the things he never
even wore or touched, but that are so, forever, his.
Maybe you dare to hope that another baby boy will
wear them. Maybe when you finally have a living baby,
your daughter, you dress her in his red T-shirt with the
gray guitar on it when you take her to music class. It's
your message to a room full of mothers who have no
real idea about what you've been through in order to
sit in a circle with them.

My son didn't die because I celebrated him. I didn't
miscarry five months later because I was too scared
to get excited or even tell my mother I was pregnant.
Fear does not protect us. So, when I could, I celebrated
my daughter while we waited for her.

I stood in front of the same red brick wall of our apartment building at 28 and 32 and 36 weeks and smiled into the camera while my husband took our picture. It's not the reason she lived. But it's the reason she can see photos of me happy while I carried her.

I let her be showered. It took weeks of fretting to finally accept a low-key luncheon a girlfriend hosted at a date far enough along that felt "safe," even though you also know better than to believe in those markers. I am grateful now, that I did, just as I am grateful that I have her brother's things, though I have managed to give some away, too. Having them hasn't made his loss harder than it already is to bear. Now, three and a half years later, it makes it a tiny bit easier to grieve. I have things to fold and refold as I think about him.

I'm pregnant for the fourth time, and I want that happiness and gratitude again for this little sister, due in April. I want even more because we are fairly certain she will be our last. So I am bonding with her with all my might. Despite fear.

If there is also that urge within you, to start a nursery now, I am here cheering you on. Nesting is a powerful, primal drive within us that even grief may not conquer. So why, dear Mama who has already lost so much, why deprive yourself of even one more ounce of joy? If you want a maternity photo shoot, give that to yourself and your baby. If you want a baby shower on your terms, talk to a close friend about how to make that happen. It will probably look different than anything you did when you were innocent, and that's OK. You are different now, and your celebrations can reflect the ways your lost baby or babies have changed you. This time, instead of clothes and gear, two friends are helping me with a "virtual shower" that will collect beads and pressed flowers from friends far and wide. I will string the beads into a necklace to hold when I need their strength. I will gather the flowers into a book my daughter can hopefully one day see as evidence of all those who sent love her way.

None of this will guarantee your baby lives, but none of it will guarantee your baby dies either. What it can guarantee is that you honor your baby while he or she is alive inside you. I know you honor him or her if you don't do these things, too. Either way, we are not waiting for them; they are already here, present, and members of our family no matter what happens. You, dear Mama, already learned that excruciating lesson.

I would love to tell you about my second daughter. She has a full name. Bright green reminds me of her. Her nursery is all but done except for washing her sister's baby clothes, a few of her brother's mixed in, and hanging a heart mobile over the rocking chair. I visualize nursing her there in the night, when it's just the two of us. I've strung her expected birthstone around my neck. It hangs with the heart I wear for her brother. She is my fourth baby, but when I picture her alive, she is playing with her sister. They are the two who, I hope, get to be here with us for the rest of our lives. My first trimester, she made me far sicker than any of her siblings. I feel like it was her way of reminding me, even then, that she is here. When I learned I was pregnant with her, the first feeling that came over me was excitement, not fear. I try to remember that whenever the fear surfaces because, of course, it does. She is already teaching me so much, just like her brother and sister have.

Dear, brave, scared, excited Mama, I would love to hear about the baby you are carrying.

I am cheering you on as you dare to bond with the baby inside. I am your biggest supporter right now because I know how much courage that requires. I'm not perfect at this. I still wait until each Thursday before I mark my calendar with a heart drawn around the number of weeks pregnant I am. This week, it will be 32. We PAL moms still take things a day at a time. Minute by minute, even, when we are waiting for our babies to kick, to assure us they are there, alive.

So maybe you are also pregnant with a first or second or third rainbow. Maybe you feel that joy bubbling up despite all you've lost. Maybe try not to listen to the voice telling you:

"It's too soon."

"Don't buy that 'little sister' onesie just yet."

"Grief doesn't allow room for joy."

"You'll have time later to be excited."

Because when is the time if not right now? While her heart is beating inside you. While he can hear yours doing the same. How connected you already are in the most undeniable way. What a cause, right there, for celebration.

I celebrate YOU, Brave Mama. I see the smile behind your fears, when it's just you and baby, your palm on your belly as it rises and falls, the glimmer in your eye as you catch your passing reflection in a window. I am smiling for you, too.

Love,

Jennifer Massoni Pardini

"My son didn't die because I celebrated him. I didn't miscarry five months later because I was too scared to get excited or even tell my mother I was pregnant. Fear does not protect us. So, when I could, I celebrated my daughter while we waited for her.

I stood in front of the same red brick wall of our apartment building at 28 and 32 and 36 weeks and smiled into the camera while my husband took our picture. It's not the reason she lived. But it's the reason she can see photos of me happy while I carried her."

Dear Courageous Mama Parenting Her Baby Born
After a Loss,

I want you to know that I am right here with you.
Right now I am 10 months into parenting my baby girl
born after my other one who died.

You know what?

I have a hard time telling you this...

But it hasn't always been easy...

And guess what?

I'm here to tell you that this is okay!

You see, I am going to share a secret with you, you
brave mama who wakes up every morning and
chooses to see the joy in this world of life after loss. So
come closer, lean into your screen as if you can hear
the keys clicking on my keyboard as I type this to you.

The secret is that "It's okay."

Yup, that is the secret and the mantra I carry with
me as I parent during this turbulent time of waltzing
between the joy and grief of this life after loss.

You see...

It's okay if when your subsequent child is born and
placed in your arms that for a moment you searched in
her face for your child that died. I know I did.

It's okay that if in those first few days of mothering this new life, this life that got to live, if you felt indifferent and almost detached from your baby after he arrived, worried about getting to attached because this baby might be taken from you too. I know I did.

It's okay that when you bring your newborn home for the first time you spend the evening crying over their tiny body, rocking back and forth and grieving, missing, and wanting your baby that died as you sing this baby to sleep. I know I did.

It's okay if you feel different from other moms who haven't experienced a loss. Even though you have a baby in your arms now doesn't mean you have forgotten the one that died. I know I haven't.

It's okay if there are days when you get so busy that for a moment or an hour or maybe two that you forget her, your child that came before this one and did not live. I know I sometimes do.

It's okay if you have a hard time moving up in size of baby clothes remembering that these clothes were originally for her, your child that died, and putting them away seems to remind you that she is not coming back and with this thought you weep uncontrollable tears of sorrow. I know I did.

It's okay if grief comes back and stays for a while. This new life is a reminder of the life that did not get to live. Grief is just your way of still loving your baby that died. I know I do.

It's okay if joy overwhelms you. Welcome the old friend back into your life. You have waited so long for her to arrive. Enjoy the moments you get to spend together. I know I do.

It's okay if anxiety and depression sneak in. This is to be expected after what you have been through. Don't judge yourself that these unwanted guest have arrived. Just breathe and reach out to a mental health therapist, doctor or midwife, and ask them where you can find support. I know I did and I still do.

It's okay if checking on your baby's breathing each night before you can fall asleep has become part of your bedtime routine. I know it is part of mine.

It's okay when your little one gets sick for the first time and you panic! Calling the doctor at odd hours of the night and praying to God that he doesn't take this one too. It is your right to do everything in your power to protect this baby from illness and, God forbid, death. I know I do.

It's okay to not be okay all the time. Parts of this life after loss and raising your baby born after the one that died are still going to be hard and sad. Just remember, it's okay to not be okay all the time. I know I'm not.

It's okay if you sleep on your child's floor each night for the first week after you move baby out of your bedroom and into the nursery. I know I did.

It's okay to open those 12 month, 18 month, and 24 month clothes in hopes that this baby will make it to that age unlike your other child. I know I do.

It's okay to still be scared. The fear of losing this child too doesn't go away in the first week, month or maybe not even the first year. You have suffered the greatest loss there is, and it makes sense if you still fear it happening again. I know I do.

It's okay to be happy when your baby rolls, walks, and talks for the first time. Embracing the good times doesn't mean you are not honoring your child that died. Actually living life to the fullest after the loss of your child is one of the greatest gifts you can give them. So when this baby coos and smiles at you, remember to welcome the joy. I know I do.

It's also okay to embrace every bit of life after loss: the love, the pain, the grief, the joy. It's okay to live in all of it. Because that is what this life is.

Just remember…It's okay.

With Love,

Lindsey Henke

Fellow PAL Mom, Courageous PAL Warrior, & Brave Parenting After Loss Mama
Mom to Nora, Zoe & Liev
LindseyMHenke.com

"It's okay if grief comes back and stays for a while. This new life is a reminder of the life that did not get to live. Grief is just your way of still loving your baby that died. I know I do.

It's okay if joy overwhelms you. Welcome the old friend back into your life. You have waited so long for her to arrive. Enjoy the moments you get to spend together. I know I do."

To The Person Who Is Pregnant After Loss,

I know I should start by congratulating you on your pregnancy, but you and I both know how complicated those congratulations can be.

While I'm happy for you, I am also worried. I'm sure you can relate. This is what it's like to be pregnant after a loss. There are a lot of feelings to maneuver. It's hard to focus on one feeling. Because when you're happy about being pregnant, you're also scared that it could end. You're excited to meet your new baby and worried that they won't survive.

All of these feelings are valid. But there are times when it's too much. And while it's not possible to completely shelve all those feelings, it is possible to hit the pause button and just focus on right now.

When things feel impossible and scary and unknown, just focus on right now.

RIGHT NOW you are pregnant.

I don't know what tomorrow holds or even the next hour, but I know that right now you are pregnant.

We both know how quickly this can change. We know how swiftly things can go from wonderful to devastating--from life to death.

But right now?

Right now you are pregnant.

Right now, inside of you, is a baby who is very much alive. A baby who is growing. A baby who is more than a possibility--they are very real.

Because RIGHT NOW, you are pregnant.

Take a moment to lean in and focus on the right now. This exact moment in time when you are pregnant. No matter what happens, no one can take away this moment. This moment is yours. It belongs to you and your baby.

What is happening right now is not a guarantee, but there is one thing I can guarantee.

The love you are feeling right now? That is forever.

Love,

Rachel

Dorothy and Frances's Mama
www.unexpectedfamilyouting.com
www.facebook.com/unexpectedfamilyouting

"RIGHT NOW, you are pregnant.

Take a moment to lean in and focus on the right now.
This exact moment in time when you are pregnant. No
matter what happens, no one can take away this moment.
This moment is yours. It belongs to you and your baby."

Dear Brave Mama,

I imagine that being called both "brave" and "mama" might fill you with emotions, as I know that you don't feel brave but rather terrified, and that you are unsure if you have earned the title of "Mama." Let me assure you that indeed, you are both. Brave for following your dreams of having a child when you know that the path isn't as seamless as you once thought. You've been a Mama since your first positive pregnancy test— no matter if that ended in the first trimester, second trimester, third trimester, after birth, or you had the blessing of a healthy child. With each pregnancy, not only is a baby built, but also a mother. We all know that our journey is filled with wounds from being a mother, as often times the road was incomplete.

Yet here you are. Walking down the road again, hoping against hope for a rainbow at the end. As I write this, I am with my two rainbows and I am struck how different I was with each of their pregnancies. My daughter came to me as my fifth pregnancy and one child. In between my living son and my daughter, I lost three pregnancies. One was early on, the second occurred at 21 weeks and the third at 19 weeks. Going into my pregnancy with my daughter I knew statistics: I had a 25% chance of miscarrying (normal odds) and I had a 25% chance of losing this pregnancy in the second trimester because of a recessive gene combination that my husband and I carry. For the latter, this wouldn't be determined definitively until I was 18 weeks.

I was told often during my daughter's pregnancy how courageous I was to continue. In fact, I didn't feel that way. I was scared, pessimistic, and doubtful that I'd ever hear my own baby's cry. I had a wonderful support network, and through them, I asked each to "carry my hope." I was unable to risk my heart and hope in this pregnancy, as I was so sure that it would also end catastrophically. The pregnancy was a blur but towards the end, I slowly started to embrace hope. I threw myself an "elephant party" as I realized that I had been gestating my daughter for what felt like the nearly 22 month that an elephant does. (In counting all of the weeks I had been pregnant leading up to this one). At that celebration, I thanked everyone who had supported me during this long road.

After my daughter was born healthy, I realized what else I had lost. I lost the innocence of pregnancy and a road devoid of any conclusion other than a healthy baby at the end. I wanted that back. When my daughter (who's middle name in Hebrew is Tikvah, which means Hope) was a year, I decided to claim it. I became pregnant again and I was in a mindset where I could accept whatever outcome that might befall me: a loss early on; a loss later on for the genetic issue; or a healthy baby. That rainbow pregnancy was such a contrast. I was able to put aside the anxiety I felt previously and relish the miracle that was occurring.

I carried the pregnancy also knowing that this would be my last one and that I wasn't only looking at the outcome, but I was really invested in my process. I was determined that I would engage and plan for a baby in terms of my birth plan, the nursery, follow up care, and having my two living children prepare with me. My second son's birth was such a contrast to his older sister. He was still a rainbow, but one that followed much less of a storm, more like the image that comes from a sunny day while playing with a running hose of water.

You, Brave Mama, can claim aspects of this pregnancy. You can call on others for hope. You can plan. You can choose not to. Loss took things from you, but you still have your voice. While you can't ultimately choose an outcome, there are so many other aspects of choice that you can embrace. They don't have to be big and they don't have to be the things that others want from you.

Know that I too, will hold your hope.

Love,

Dr. Julie Bindeman

Mother to Baby Boy, Baby Girl, Nate, Jordan and Ryan

"I had a wonderful support network, and through them, I asked each to "carry my hope." I was unable to risk my heart and hope in this pregnancy, as I was so sure that it would also end catastrophically."

Dear Mama,

There is so much that I wish I could say to you to take away the anxiety and fear that you most likely feel. I am not sure where you are at in the pregnancy, if you're 8 weeks, 12 weeks, 20 weeks, or almost to the end. Depending on your loss(es), that may determine how you are feeling right now.

For me, as soon as I found out I was pregnant via frozen embryo transfer, I needed to shout it from the rooftops. Maybe you're hiding your pregnancy, or maybe you're like me and needed to feel connected in order to keep sane. No matter what you feel – it's completely normal. To me, I had to really embrace it in order to make it feel real. Even then, it felt surreal all the time – that I was carrying a baby, that this baby would only know their brother as our angel.

This isn't to say I wasn't still scared of everything – every twitch that didn't feel right, every headache, every symptom that became slightly less, and every ultrasound that I went to thinking my baby wouldn't have a heartbeat that time. In my 8 years in the loss community, I've learned (and you probably have to) terms that I never knew existed; conditions that sound straight out of a medical reference book. At ultrasounds, I would ask a million questions, questions that made the ultrasound techs question if I worked in the medical field. I just knew all the horror stories.

But, I knew the beautiful stories as well of life after loss – of pregnancy after loss when everything turns out perfect and there is a living breathing baby. I am here to tell you that you CAN be scared and fearful while at the same time embrace your pregnancy and have happy moments. You are growing a baby(ies) inside of you – creating a sibling for your baby.

While you may think your new baby won't know about their brother or sister, you can make sure that they will – by telling them about their brother or sister. As I sit here with my beautiful rainbow on my lap – on my son's angelversary, I can tell you that your heart can feel full and feel like something is missing all at the same time. But, when your rainbow smiles at you – and looks just like their angel sibling – your heart feels complete knowing that they're both with you – no matter how far away heaven may feel.

Keep rockin' this pregnancy, like the rockstar you are. You've got this.

Sending you love & dragonflies,

Shannon Bensalah

Cameron & Ellie's Mom

"I am here to tell you that you CAN be scared and fearful while at the same time embrace your pregnancy and have happy moments."

Dear Superhero Mama Parenting After Loss,

You have to hear this. You are doing a great job.
A phenomenal job.

Parenting is hard work no matter what your journey to
get there looks like. But this parenting after loss gig,
I am willing to bet it's even tougher. Because I don't
think I would have half of the fears lurking in my head
if I hadn't lost five babies before birthing a healthy
breathing one. My most traumatic loss, which resulted
in giving birth to my deceased yet perfect baby boy
at 28 weeks, has taught me quite a few things about
control. Mainly that we have very little of it.

But then here we are, parenting a living, laughing,
squishy little baby. It's the most amazing thing in the
world. The most wondrous and beautiful of emotions
possible. The extreme opposite of grief, which is pure
joy.

And then, we are forced to make decisions for these
little babies. Ones we never had to before.

> "Should we co-sleep? I can't, I might hurt my
> baby.
>
> Do we breastfeed? I have to, it will keep my
> baby healthy and alive.
>
> Do I vaccinate?
>
> What about SIDS?

Do I get a monitoring device for when she is sleeping? Will that make it worse?

Do I treat this fever or let her immune system grow?

Should I rock her all night or sleep train her?

Solid food? What if she chokes?

Stuffy nose? But what if she can't breathe?

Play groups? But it's cold and flu season.

Take a night out for myself? But what if something happens to her?

Tune out for 20 minutes? I can't, what if she passes away and I never get another 20 minutes again?"

I know. It's insanely hard, Mama.

I can hear inside your head because I am you. I think it would be hard on any Mom but let's be honest, we got the crummy end of the stick in ways. Our minds are not capable of going back to a time that felt safe and predictable. So let me tell you this.

You are not crazy. You are not a helicopter Mom. You are not neurotic or a germa-phob. You are not too overprotective. You don't ask the pediatrician too many questions. You don't analyze too much. You aren't losing your mind.

You are parenting after loss.

You are walking through this uncharted territory that there are no baby books about. And if it's anything like my journey, not many people understand the see-saw of emotions you bounce between several times per day. Only a select handful of people understand that you not only suffered loss(es) but you endured real trauma.

The mind takes time to figure that stuff out. So be easy on yourself. Remember that it's okay to think about your other child and feel sad. This does not mean you aren't grateful for your living child. It's okay to be scared, you've been through something really scary. It's okay to ask for help or need time to yourself. You are human and need to pour into yourself in order to pour back into your children, no matter where they are. It's okay if the first thing you did on Christmas morning was shed tears. Your holiday was missing something, something irreplaceable. And it's just as okay that 20 minutes later you were laughing and smiling next the Christmas tree with your living baby.

I can assume that your mind has been consumed with the thoughts of a future baby as well.

"Can I really do this pregnancy thing all over again? Am I strong enough, am I willing to risk it?" I know that this baby was more than worth the stressful pregnancy, but if you decide you don't want to do it again, that doesn't somehow negate that. Nor does it mean that the baby you lost wasn't "worth it." I promise. You don't have to know what you want to do. And it's okay to be confused about it. Try not to compare yourself to other PAL Moms. This is your journey. You don't have to have more than one living child to be courageous. Just like you don't have to have more than one loss to be heartbroken.

One more thing...

You are enough for your baby. You are more than enough. You were specifically chosen, hand-picked in fact to be your baby's mother. You. Because you are more than capable, more than worthy and perfectly suited for that little squishy being. You mama, are incredible. Parenting children in two different universes takes superhero strength.

You are a superhero mama.

I see your invisible cape because I am wearing one too.

Lisa Hand

Jake Edward Hand's Mama
tobecalledmama.com

"You are not crazy. You are not a helicopter Mom. You are not neurotic or a germa-phob. You are not too overprotective. You don't ask the pediatrician too many questions. You don't analyze too much. You aren't losing your mind.

You are parenting after loss."

Dear Mama...Your Baby's Light Is In There

Can you see her light? When you lie in bed at night and close your eyes and put your hands on your belly, do you see it shining out from inside you? Are you letting her light expand, grow and fill you, so that you glow with the joy of pregnancy you used to believe enveloped every woman with a baby inside her?

Or, has the blackness of grief that lives inside you blanketed that light with it's heaviness and fear?

That was the image that remains most etched into my head and heart around my rainbow pregnancy. A vision I had while lying in bed one night shortly after learning I was pregnant. I envisioned a ray of light, so tiny and so bright and pure, trying to break it's way through the ashes of death that lived beneath my skin.

I didn't want my daughter to grow in me, in that. But I was in grief, and I knew I needed to honor that as well.

I decided that night to make a choice. I could not make my grief "go away," nor did I want to, so I would allow it into my life with open arms. And I would also seek out light. I would proactively look for joy, fun, laughter. I would reach through the darkness inside of me to nurture the light that needed space to grow.

And that's when I started wearing sequins.

I'd given away all of my old maternity clothes. I couldn't bear to look at them. When I went to buy new clothes I turned towards items that were going to reflect my daughters light and connect to her. I wore little black, brown or gray (except when covered in sparkles.)

It was hard at first. For years I'd been walking around in the shadows. Allowing myself to stay invisible in clothes that allowed me to disappear behind them. I, like so many others, was used to walking the aisles of whatever clothing store, eyeing a beautifully bold colored sweater and then buying it in black or gray. Now, for the sake of my little bean of light, I bought it in a color. A color that made me smile.

Now, I'm not saying that what you wear is the holy grail of having a joyful, easy rainbow pregnancy.

It's far from it.

But it helps. It helps to know your baby's light is in there. It helps to know that you CAN reach out to it, nurture it and love it. Despite the fear.

And the fear was huge.

I didn't share my rainbow pregnancy online until she was just about here.

I had a panic attack at 27 weeks at a bus station in midtown Manhattan because I didn't feel her kick for a few hours, even after drinking an entire glass of orange juice. As soon as I felt her movement, I was OK, yet I spent that day in a local teaching hospital getting examined inside and out by more people than I care to admit.

I accepted that it was par for the course and that I had a right to be scared. Hiding from my feelings wasn't going to make me feel them any less.

As my due date drew closer my fear multiplied many times over. I spent time online, trying to avoid loss sites yet somehow finding myself always on them. Suddenly everywhere I turned I was seeing comments from women with late losses. They bombarded me and I went online and rented a doppler so I could hear my little one's heartbeat whenever I got nervous.

It helped.

Dear mama, there is no right or wrong when it comes to pregnancy after loss. There are no rules to follow or mind games you can play with yourself.

Just feel. Feel the pain, the fear, the grief the sadness. But also feel the joy, the beauty, the promise and the light. They are all there for you. And though the former seem to find you no matter what you are doing, the latter require effort. They require thought and intention.

But they are worth the effort. Your babies light shines out through you. Just find a way to build a doorway for her.

Loads of love,

Tova Gold

Mom to Sunshine and Daisy, Molly and Liat

"I decided that night to make a choice. I could not make my grief "go away," nor did I want to, so I would allow it into my life with open arms. And I would also seek out light. I would proactively look for joy, fun, laughter. I would reach through the darkness inside of me to nurture the light that needed space to grow."

To The Mom Expecting Again After Loss,

I was you not too long ago, and hopefully one day,
I'll be you again. First and foremost, it's okay to cry.
I cried most of my pregnancy after loss too. It's been
almost two years since my pregnancy after loss ended
and my daughter was placed in my arms, ALIVE.

I wasn't ever sure if we'd get there. To be honest, I had
her funeral planned before her nursery. Down to every
detail, her funeral was planned.

I'm a planner by nature, you see. I have a need to
plan everything I can ahead of time. So either way
my pregnancy ended, I would be prepared. The easy
thing for me to plan was her funeral - it was what I
knew. Planning for what happens after you give birth,
that I was not good at. My plans the first time never
ended in a funeral for one of my twins, nor did they
include surgeries and the NICU. So with my daughter's
pregnancy, I was prepared for her funeral.

But I also wanted to be prepared for bringing her
home, too. And that thought was so scary. I knew I
couldn't do it. So I called my mom. I let my mom get
excited about my pregnancy because I couldn't. She
put her room together and washed her clothes, and
did all the things I couldn't do. I bought two things for
my daughter, both of which I figured we could use at
her funeral, as well as if she was born alive: a blanket,
and a onsie with her name embroidered on it.

I think it's okay to only be able to do what you can
handle. So many people kept telling me 'everything

will be alright this time, don't worry.' Those people don't know what we know. We know death. We know the weight of our lifeless children in our arms, or what it feels like when the doctor says there is no heartbeat. WE know, and they do not.

Every morning I woke up scared that would be the day it was all over, and every night I went to sleep begging my baby to give me just one more kick so I knew she was alive. My friend lent me her doppler and I listened to my daughter's heartbeat for hours, sometimes I just had it on along with the TV, just so I knew her heart was still beating. That doppler kept me sane those months.

If you can't handle a baby shower or baby gifts, don't have one and ask for people not to give you any. I had my mom stockpile things at her house because I knew I just couldn't handle it. I know that people will tell you to believe and faith - but I also know how hard it is to believe and have faith. If you can't do those things, it's okay.

I didn't.

And it's really hard to admit, but I could never 'see' myself with my daughter. I could only see a funeral.

I can tell you that it's worth it. Every pain, every ache, every ounce of fear is worth it. What was supposed to be my 'happy ending' to my son's death ended in an emergency D&C. We miscarried at 10 weeks in the most awful, drawn out way of loss in the first trimester. For several weeks we were told to 'have hope and pray' but our baby never grew and we never saw a heartbeat.

I can tell you that I was done trying. I lost my hope and I truly thought I would never have more than my surviving twin. I thought he was my 'fluke' healthy baby and that I was never really meant to be a mother. My husband convinced me to keep trying with fertility medicine until we ran out of money. The very next time we attempted IUI, we found out we were pregnant on Friday the 13th.

I laughed.

When our daughter was born 9 months later on Friday the 13th, I shook with fear in the OR. I was actually shaking so hard they couldn't give me a spinal tap. A wonderful, amazing nurse wiped my tears and held my hands and asked me my son's name.

It's okay if your delivery is wrapped in fear. I asked the anesthesiologist about 80 times if she was breathing even though I could hear her cries. The fact that she was alive never really hit me until she was placed in my arms.

And it was beautiful. Those moments in which I experienced what so many women take for granted were so beautiful. And worth it. Worth every tear, every minute of being scared and all of the heartache that entailed the miscarriage the year prior. I'd go through all the fear again to have my daughter. She healed me in ways I can't explain.

She was truly, truly a gift. And your baby will be, too. Even if right now, you're not sure that gift will ever come home alive.

Sincerely,

Megan Skaggs

A Mom Who Has Survived Pregnancy After Loss.

"I think it's okay to only be able to do what you can handle. So many people kept telling me 'everything will be alright this time, don't worry.' Those people don't know what we know. We know death. We know the weight of our lifeless children in our arms, or what it feels like when the doctor says there is no heartbeat. WE know, and they do not."

Dearest Mumma,

You are so brave. I know you probably don't think you are, but please know that you are braver than you realize. If you're anything like me, your pregnancy after loss is the hardest thing you have done since you said goodbye to your precious baby. I became pregnant just ten short weeks after my daughter was stillborn. Never had I felt such a strange mix of emotions – I was elated to know that at least one of my children was alive but I was so very scared that I was going to experience another loss. It takes courage to have another baby after loss; it takes bravery to face each new day. Pregnancy after loss is a long journey and you, sweet mumma, are the bravest of all mothers.

It wasn't until I reached the end of my pregnancy that I realised just how much it had affected me. I look at photos from those 38 weeks and cannot help but notice the glazed look and bags under my eyes. I'm not sure that there was even a single moment of that pregnancy when I felt at peace. There were glimpses of hope, but they were always tainted with worry and instead of finding joy in moments such as hearing a heartbeat, all I felt was relief. It felt as though I could finally let out my breath, but only for a moment, because I knew there was no guarantee that the heartbeat would be there the next day. To be pregnant when you know there is no guarantee of a living child at the end of it makes you so very brave.

I wish I could give you some advice, some words of wisdom to help you along this difficult road. But I don't know that I can. I wish I could say that I thrived during my pregnancy, that I bonded with the baby straight away and made the most of each moment. But I can't. I wish I could say that my Christian faith and trust in God was enough to give me peace and comfort during those long 38 weeks. But it didn't. All I did for 38 weeks was survive. Sometimes surviving looked like an anxious mum-to-be, calling my midwife because something small had me concerned or going to hospital to be monitored for peace of mind. At other times, surviving looked more like collapsing in a heap, running into my bedroom to curl up on my bed and hide from the world and while crying endless tears on my husband's shoulder.

I suppose the only advice I can offer is to do what you need to do. If you need to hear a heartbeat, call your midwife or go to the hospital. Don't worry about inconveniencing them, it is their job to help you through your pregnancy. If you need to fall apart emotionally, give yourself the grace to do so. Visit a special spot, go for a walk, listen to calming music or curl up on your bed and don't feel guilty for allowing yourself some time. A pregnancy after loss does not take away the pain or grief from your loss and there is no need pretend that it does. Be honest with what you need and then meet those needs. I know that above all, you need your baby to be with you safely. But since we cannot know that until they are born, try to meet your other needs. You are strong. You are brave. You can do this.

As I sit here and gaze at my three week old son, I cannot help but think that the stress, sleeplessness, and anxiety were worth it. A precious baby boy safely in my arms; a child of my own who is alive. And my hope is that you too will have a living child at the end of this pregnancy. Hold on, dear mumma, one day at a time, your baby is getting closer.

With love,

Larissa Genat

Mom of Ariella, Levi, Seanna, Amos, and Caleb
loveisdeeperstill.blogspot.com
facebook.com/loveisdeeperstill

"To be pregnant when you know there is no guarantee of a living child at the end of it makes you so very brave."

Dear Pregnant Bereaved Mother,

I am sorry that you lost your child.

I'm sorry that losing your child caused you to lose your naivety about pregnancy.

I'm sorry that the world of child loss was opened to you.

I'm sorry that you know there truly is no "safe zone" with pregnancy.

I'm sorry that you weren't as excited with this positive test as you were with the one before loss.

I'm sorry that you felt guilty about that fact.

I'm sorry that your experience is now clouded by fear and anxiety.

I'm sorry that this is your reality.

Pregnancy after loss (PAL) with my twin daughters is the second hardest thing I've been through; the first being losing my son, Asher.

Every day the fear of "would this be our last day together" was there. The fact that we had no explanation for why Asher died in utero plagued me every day. There was nothing different to be done in this pregnancy to prevent the same outcome from happening. I struggled to allow myself to be excited because I was fearful they would die like their brother.

I became obsessive with counting their kicks. I marked each one in an app on my phone from the moment I woke to the moment I went to sleep. I would lie awake at 3:00am waiting to go back to bed until I felt movement from each baby. I was heavily monitored with bi-weekly ultrasounds throughout my pregnancy. The reassurance after each appointment never lasted long. Once that wand was off my belly, the fear of the unknown in my own body set in.

I became a master of delusion. I would tell myself "one day at a time" and forced myself to focus on the present; today my daughters were dancing in my belly, today they were still alive. I refused to allow myself to look into the future, to dream of them coming home with us. The idea of preparing for babies who may never come home was too much for my already broken heart.

My advice to you as you journey through pregnancy after loss?

Do what you need to do to get through it. Pregnancy after loss is a complete and utter mindf**k. It is something you need to get through in order to get to the desired outcome of, hopefully, bringing home a living child. For me, that meant not focusing on the due date but just focusing on each day.

Surround yourself with physicians who understand the fear and anxiety pregnancy after loss brings. Find doctors who are going to be understanding when you call for every ache and pain and want to be seen "just to be sure." Two of my Maternal Fetal Medicine doctors are members of the loss community. They knew all too well my feelings of anxiety so they were always willing to help ease it in whatever way they possibly could.

Advocate for yourself and your baby. Don't be afraid to make that call on the weekend for reduced fetal movement. Don't be afraid to call for the unusual side pain. Don't be afraid to call. Push for the care you and your baby need, even if it's not medically necessary in the doctor's eyes. If you need to be seen every two weeks to get through this pregnancy, then you need to find doctors who will do that. You know yourself and your body best, don't be afraid to give a little push back.

Find someone you can lean on during this time, someone who has been through PAL or is going through it, someone who "gets it." Non-loss friends struggle to understand the complicated feelings that come along with PAL which can leave you feeling isolated. Finding someone who has been there eases those feelings of loneliness. I walked through pregnancy after loss with a fellow loss mother at the same exact time. Having someone to share that experience with, who understood the anxiety I was feeling, was invaluable. We got through our pregnancies after loss with the help of on another.

Every kick, every flutter, every ultrasound photo, embrace it all. Try your best to cherish every moment because you know all too well how quickly things can change.

Remember you CAN do this and that you are NEVER alone in it.

In Love and Loss,

Amy Lied

Asher, Harper, and Scarlett's Mama
http://www.doggiebagsnotdiaperbags.wordpress.com/

"My advice to you as you journey through pregnancy after loss?

Do what you need to do to get through it. Pregnancy after loss is a complete and utter mindf**k. It is something you need to get through in order to get to the desired outcome of, hopefully, bringing home a living child. For me, that meant not focusing on the due date but just focusing on each day."

Dear Brave Heart,

Is it okay if I call you that? Because you totally are.
Bringing in new life after facing unthinkable loss,
takes courage all it's own. Courage and new love.
Transformation. It will be some of the hardest work
you will ever, ever do. But I don't have to tell you that
it will all be worth it.

It's been a little over a year since we brought home
our second rainbow and four and half years since we
lost our first child. She was a girl and born 11 weeks
early. Since then we've had two NICU "rainbow"
children. None of this has been a cakewalk. I've heard
everything from "Why aren't you happy about this?"
(referring to my pregnancy) to "you're finally getting
your girl!!" I think it is safe to say that our friends
and family try, but they might as well be walking on
eggshells because there is pretty much nothing you
can say that doesn't NOW have a different meaning.
None of those phrases were meant to hurt, but they
did.

Aside from the comments, my first rainbow pregnancy
was an absolute disaster. It was terror-filled. To the
brim. I can hardly remember details - only that I did
not allow any space for joy. I didn't intentionally shun
it, there just wasn't any room for it, does that make
sense? It was awful.

So, I wrote a book on it when I fell pregnant with
my second "rainbow" child. I didn't realize that my
pregnancy was filled with that much terror until I
tried to remember it, and couldn't. It was like one
big blur. It made my heart ache. This might sound

contradictory, but all in all, I really do love to be pregnant – the kicks, the tummy growing, feeling the baby move and my word, the heartbeat!!! Pregnancy is SUCH a miracle! So when I couldn't remember my pregnancy with our first "rainbow" child, I made a pact with myself that this would be a fear-free and guilt-free zone this go-around. This was a gift to myself, and to my newest child. I would enjoy her. I wanted to remember this. I deserved this.

And YOU. DO. TOO.

I am big on mantras. You can write something on a Post-It note that encourages your heart in the right way and affirms your decision to enjoy this pregnancy, and maybe stick it on your mirror so you run into it every morning. Or set yourself little random reminders on your phone. Be intentional. Guilt and fear will be, so you have to be vigilant.

One thing I super-struggled with, with my first "rainbow" pregnancy was guilt. Oh my word, the guilt. I felt like I was flat-out betraying my daughter we had buried only months before (four to be exact). What right did I have to be happy again? Did I even know how to be happy? Did I want to be happy!? I wanted a baby. More than anything in this world, but this was the epitome of bittersweet. Choosing between life and death.

The real hard facts are that we have the rest of our lives to grieve for the children we will never hold again, but we only have a very small window in time to grow this new life and allow ourselves to be swallowed up in new motherhood once again. It is a sacred journey. And one you don't have to travel alone.

You deserve this, Brave Heart Mama. So find your mantra. Words that help your heart each morning and throughout the day, and let them minister to you – to shun out the fear and guilt and make room for the joy that is yours for the taking.

Franchesca Cox

"The real hard facts are that we have the rest of our lives to grieve for the children we will never hold again, but we only have a very small window in time to grow this new life and allow ourselves to be swallowed up in new motherhood once again. It is a sacred journey. And one you don't have to travel alone."

Dear Mother-Who-Is-Pulled-In-Two-Directions,

Pregnancy after a loss is a special time and a challenging time. Grief and hormones send you on a roller coaster of emotions. Constantly pulled in two directions, you want to be excited and happy about the child growing inside you, but want to honour and cherish the child that came before. You can't quite enjoy the moment, trying to strike the balance between hope for the future and grief for what has been lost. And all the usual sources of advice; the parenting web sites, friends and family, pregnancy books, and even your doctor/midwife just aren't able to address your needs. Like a shoe that doesn't fit, their suggestions feel uneasy and uncomfortable. "Just relax!" Oh, how I hated those words!

Of course, it isn't just well-meaning family and friends who put their foot in their mouth. Sometimes even health care professionals, who are aware of our history and ought to know better, are the ones who say the wrong things. One medical resident, when I came for an emergency consult (turns out I had pneumonia!), looked at my chart and said "Boy, you'll be busy with 5 kids at home!" The minute she opened her mouth, she knew what she'd said was wrong, and I know she felt terrible. Doctors are humans too and in her rush to see me for my immediate problem – I couldn't breathe – she forgot to think about my other concern: that my first three pregnancies ended in loss.

Do I have advice for women traveling this journey of pregnancy after a loss? Maybe. Each of us has a slightly different experience, a slightly different story to tell. We can learn so much from one another.

I recently starting thinking about how we can develop a better relationship with our health care professionals. These are just my suggestions:

1. When booking your first appointment, ask the receptionist if you can have a little extra time. It might only be 5 minutes, but it will help ensure that you can get your questions answered and not feel rushed.

2. Practice what you want to say beforehand. Write it down and read it aloud to a friend or your partner. By practicing in advance, you'll feel more comfortable telling your story and they can give you tips on how to make it better.

3. Bring a pen and paper to appointments and write down any questions you have. If there are words you are unfamiliar with, you can ask them to write them down so you can look them up later.

4. If you want to, bring your partner or a friend to your appointments. They can catch things you miss and may be able to remember things you've forgotten.

5. Remember your doctor / midwife isn't psychic! Be sure to tell them about your concerns, and about any herbal or natural medicines you're taking. They've heard it all before and shouldn't judge you.

6. Ask if you can communicate via e-mail. More

and more doctors are comfortable with this and sometimes it is easier to write things than say it to their faces, especially if you're emotional or embarrassed.

The best relationships are built on a foundation of good communication and trust. When you've experienced a loss, that trust is often broken, even if you don't blame your doctor or midwife for the death of your child. Your faith in a healthy pregnancy has been shattered. If you're feeling uneasy with the care you're getting, let them know. How they respond will hopefully make the trusting a little easier. Whatever you do, be kind to yourself and kind to others. It goes a long way toward making the world a better place.

With love,

Amanda Ross-White

Mother to Nathaniel, Samuel, Rebecca and Alexander
Joyattheendoftherainbow.com

""Just relax!" Oh, how I hated those words!"

Dear Courageous Mama who feels like a Ticking Time Bomb,

Mama, will you sit and chat with me for a bit? I'm having a rest on the couch and would love the company. Grab a cup of tea and prop yourself up on some pillows.

What's happening right now in your pregnancy after loss? Are you starting fertility treatments? Are you on bedrest after having testing or getting a cerclage placed? Were you just diagnosed with preeclampsia? Do the doctors have concerns about your or your baby? Do you have gestational diabetes? Are things going relatively well in your pregnancy, but you still feel a nagging that there is something wrong?

Pregnancy after loss is so very hard for even the most textbook of pregnancies. We mamas wince at every pain and panic when we don't feel movement for 15 minutes. We hold our breath before every appointment and ultrasound. It feels like we're holding a ticking time bomb without a visible countdown clock. We hope and pray that the bomb doesn't go off, that it's dismantled in time to give birth to our babies – alive and healthy.

Mama, I've been there. While the first two trimesters of my pregnancy after loss were anxiety-producing, they were actually fairly uneventful and "textbook." But, that changed at 32 weeks when I was hospitalized for gestational hypertension after my blood pressure was incredibly high at my weekly OB appointment. My OB worried that I had crossed from gestational hypertension to preeclampsia. She warned me that I might not be going home, and my baby may have to be delivered early.

After a weekend in the hospital being monitored, I was discharged with no signs of preeclampsia. But the maternal fetal medicine specialist gave me instructions to take it easy. He told me to think of myself as a "lady of leisure" on house rest, not quite bed rest. We met with a NICU doctor to find out what we could expect if we delivered early. I went home, and the countdown and ticking began.

Mamas, we live in constant fear of that other shoe dropping. We expect that it will happen. I almost felt validated when I was hospitalized. "See! I knew something was wrong! And I let my guard down because I accepted that I was having a textbook pregnancy," I thought. But, Mama, I'm here to tell you that it doesn't work that way.

We know better than anyone how fragile life is, how no guarantees exist. We cling to what little we can control, because we know that 99.9% of what happens through our pregnancy is completely out of our control. We set conditions on our preparation for baby—trying to protect the baby, as well as our hearts. We don't install the car seats or pack our hospital bags, fearing that will be an immediate death sentence for our precious babies. We wait to announce the pregnancy and ask our friends and family to wait until after the baby is born to host our baby showers. We approach every baby purchase and preparation task with abundant caution.

But, those conditions and cautions? They don't

determine whether or not our babies survive. They may protect us a bit. They may give us back a little of the control we feel like we have lost. But they won't change the outcome for our babies, because that is completely out of our control. So, we make conditions, protect our hearts, and bond the best that we can, all while hearing the ticking time bomb in the background. It's no wonder we're balls of anxiety.

For those last few weeks of my pregnancy, I put all my energy in dismantling that ticking time bomb myself. I tested fate and attended two baby showers for babe and me. I even bought a new dress for the shower. And, you know what? My baby kept on kicking.

We attended childbirth classes, which helped my husband and I both feel more prepared and supported for the birth of our baby, no matter the outcome. We talked to, read to, and sang to our baby. Because of the gestational hypertension, I had weekly biophysical profile ultrasounds, and I actually began to look forward to those appointments. They were an extra chance to see our precious baby on that screen and add more images to the scrapbook, rather than how I dreaded ultrasounds earlier in the pregnancy. I tried to embrace my "house rest," because I knew that was what was best for babe and me.

Mama, this takes WORK, but so does the worry and anxiety. Did my worry and anxiety go away? Absolutely not! Even now with my daughter here, living and thriving, I don't think they will ever fully go away. But, I tried to enjoy the moments while I could. And, when you can't hold onto hope, ask someone to do it for you. Have them write you a note, or write the baby a note, and tape it to your bathroom mirror. I clung to a wish for the baby from one of my dear friends at my baby shower, "Dear Baby, I hope you never forget that you are loved and treasured—an answer to many prayers."

Mama, I know how much you love this baby, no matter how guarded you are. Your fear doesn't erase your love. Hope is the only way to dismantle the bomb. Let your love and hope rise when it can. And when you can't summon it, remember we are here loving and hoping for you and your baby too. You ARE a courageous mama! Even courageous mamas need a little extra love and support. I hope you can feel that today and each day as you travel the journey of pregnancy after loss.

Much love,

Valerie Meek

Mama to Patrick and Elsbeth
MeekManor.com
facebook.com/meekmanor
instagram.com/meekmanor

"Mama, I know how much you love this baby, no matter how guarded you are. Your fear doesn't erase your love. Hope is the only way to dismantle the bomb. Let your love and hope rise when it can. And when you can't summon it, remember we are here loving and hoping for you and your baby too."

Dear Loss Mom Considering Options Other Than Pregnancy,

I can empathize with how you're feeling. You have suffered a huge loss or maybe even multiple losses, maybe even had your life at risk, and been told pregnancy is still a possibility, but one that terrifies you. You have questioned everything you know, probably thought you were less of a mom, maybe even less than a woman. It may be that right now, you have not breathed a word of these feelings to anyone, that they exist in the dark part of your mind where you hide them from the world. It may be that you have just started to talk about those feelings.

I assure you first that the feelings are completely normal and secondly that it is not true, that you are the best mom you can be, you are nothing less just because of choosing, or even considering, a different path to your next child.

I battled with all of these feelings, afraid to say a word for the longest time because how could I talk about just how badly I wanted a child at home while also saying that the idea of being pregnant terrified me. Anytime that I was even a second late, instead of the normal oh I hope this is it, I panicked, thinking about my safety, how many times I could tempt fate, risk my life, and even if it was normal, how could I deal with the anxiety of another pregnancy? When we tried another round of IVF and failed, my husband was devastated and I was relieved. I could not get pregnant, not just physically anymore, but also mentally. Everything scared me too much, it was almost a crippling fear of being pregnant. All the joy or anticipated joy was gone and in its place fear and anxiety that made me freeze. I thought about how terrible of a person I was, how terrible of a wife and a mother. I thought about women who were told that they could not get pregnant and how I was never told that, so how could I not get pregnant again, to use the God given right and opportunity that was came solely as a virtue of being lucky enough to be born female?

But, as most things, I have realized that our inner dialogue is often more judgmental and hurtful than the dialogue given out in the world. I started to realize that when I could tell other loss moms that their choice of pathways like adoption or egg donation meant they were incredible moms, that they were strong for realizing that even though they may have wanted to bring a child home in a more traditional way, they were preparing for another pathway. I also realized that is a problem we have as women and as moms, we are harder on ourselves than we are on others. I assure you that if you step back for a moment and think about what you are saying to yourself in your head, the self-judgment, the criticism, and think about saying that to a friend, you would probably say you would never do it. So why do we talk to ourselves like that? Why can't we have the confidence and self-assurance to talk to ourselves the way we would talk to our best friend?

Being a mom is not something that comes easy to most people. While we are told by everyone throughout our lives how easy it is to get pregnant and have a baby, we all know the honest and difficult truth. Even tougher, we have all lived that experience of being pregnant or having a baby and then losing that child.

The statistics prove that our experiences are not unique to us. One in eight couples trying to conceive will have infertility issues and one in four pregnant women will lose a pregnancy.

The rest of the world may not always feel the same way, but I am here to tell you that if you are reading this thinking about options after loss, you are already a mom and you are an incredible mom because parenting a non-living child is so incredibly difficult.

Being a mom and loving your child does not happen just because you carry your child. Right now, as we await the birth of our second child and hopefully the first child we will bring home, I can assure you that although I am not pregnant, I love our unborn child so much and I would risk my life for our child. The love we have to give our children does not just come from the experience of pregnancy, it comes from deep inside and grows no matter who carries the child.

So whichever pathway you choose, you are an incredible mom, you are brave, you have so much love to give, and your future child is very lucky to have you as a mom. Wishing you strength, patience, and love as you make the decision and follow the pathway.

Michelle Valiukenas

Mom to Colette Louise Tisdahl and Sweet Pea Tisdahl
www.colettelouise.com
facebook.com/colettetisdahl/
instagram.com/colettelouisetisdahl/

"The love we have to give our children does not just come from the experience of pregnancy, it comes from deep inside and grows no matter who carries the child."

To the Mother keeping her rainbow pregnancy a secret

I want you to know that I understand and your secret is safe with me.

I was right where you were, so I know how much it takes for you to be brave right now. What you have been through was traumatic. And still is. It took so much from you to make it to this point and it is okay if you are scared. We all were.

How are you feeling? Are you angry, Mama? Are you wondering how anyone could ask you to do this again? Or are you cautiously excited? Whatever the answer is, you are right to feel that way.

I remember thinking then that I couldn't trust my own body yet, so how could I ever trust anyone else with this secret? Are you wondering if you could trust those around you too?

You want to tell the world but the world didn't stand by you when you were at your most vulnerable. I understand, Mama. I want you to know that we are standing with you no matter what happens next.

I see you smiling to yourself, despite your better judgment. You know you shouldn't feel joy yet but it's creeping into you. I can see it.

Are you unconsciously touching your belly right now? Careful, Mama, you might give your secret away. But isn't it amazing how protective you already feel? Maybe even more so this time around.

Do you dare enter that baby store and look at baby clothes or is it too soon for you? It's okay if it is too soon, you can come back to it later, and maybe then there will be a super sale on just for you.

Oh Mama, is that guilt you're feeling now? I know it can be confusing feeling like you are in two places at once but I promise you, neither place is permanent. And you are headed to a most beautiful place. A place where you love and honor the life that was by living and loving the life that is.

Is the morning sickness better or worst this time around? Tell me, are you taking care of yourself love? Are you eating well and staying hydrated? Are you rested?

Are your regular clothes growing tight yet? Is this the furthest along you have ever been to?
Will you be sticking with your old doctor or do you think a change will be better for you? I decided to change doctors and instantly loved my new OBGYN. Do you feel loved and supported by your doctor?

Did you take any pictures yet? I was too afraid to take any pictures during my rainbow pregnancies but now I take pictures of them all the time. I don't want to miss a single moment and you won't want to either.

There is so much I want to tell you, but this is your journey. You have to take each step as you see fit, but just know you do not have to take it alone. You can find your tribe of Mamas just like you, who have walked the same road you are on now. We are cheering for you, praying for you and waiting for you to join us.

So I will keep your secret for as long as you need me to, and when you are ready to share with the world I will celebrate with you. Not only for the precious life you are carrying but I will celebrate you. For looking fear in the face and announcing to the world that you are not broken. For your resilience and strength. I will raise my glass to you for learning to trust your body and your instincts and for asking the hard questions and not taking no for answer.

Mostly I will celebrate you for doing all that you can to protect your baby. Without expensive car seats and baby proofing tools, you are protecting your child and he or she is so very lucky to call you Mama.

Love and Light,

Natasha Carlow

Mama to angel babies Kaden and Kai, and Kory, and to earth children Kyleigh and Caspian
facebook.com/natashacarlowauthor
Instagram.com/natashamelissacarlow
Natashacarlow.com

"So I will keep your secret for as long as you need me to, and when you are ready to share with the world I will celebrate with you. Not only for the precious life you are carrying but I will celebrate you. For looking fear in the face and announcing to the world that you are not broken."

Brave Mama,

You have worked so hard to get to where you are, pregnant with a baby you hope to finally be able to bring home. I know how scary this is. It is terrifying. Others, who are lucky to have not endured what you have, see pregnancy as joyful and this baby as a guarantee. You do not see this baby as a guarantee. You know better than that. Your history has taught you that pregnancies don't always go the way you expect them to and that babies don't always come home.

Mama, I know how hard you have worked for this. I have been there. I am sure it has been years. Perhaps you have had recurrent losses. Perhaps you experienced difficulties becoming pregnant. Maybe you underwent fertility treatment and genetic testing. Perhaps you are still using medications every day to maintain this pregnancy. Maybe you used a sperm or egg donor, or perhaps you aren't pregnant yourself but are using a gestational carrier.

Whatever the specifics of your story, you have worked hard for this. You have waited and hoped and literally put your blood, sweat, and tears into this baby. It feels like you have everything riding on this pregnancy.

I know that more than anything you want to be able to believe like those around you who have not experienced such loss. You want to have it not be a question whether this baby will be born alive, come home safely with you, and stay alive. But mama, it's okay to be afraid. It's okay to be scared.

You have been on the wrong side of the statistics

before. Your body, mind, and soul know the pain. Despite this, you have chosen to try again. Your desire to parent a living child is stronger than your fear. You have chosen to take the risk of devastation all over again because you hope it will all be worth it.

You feel like you need to be cautious and on edge to keep yourself safe, to prepare for another loss, and to brace yourself for the hurt. But what you and I both know is that nothing can brace you for the hurt of losing your child and your hopes and dreams along with them. I wish I could promise that this will not happen again, but the reality is that if the worst happens, you will survive it just like you have survived the unimaginable. And if that happens, I will be there for you, mama. We, your fellow loss moms, will be there for you. We will weep with you and grieve with you and support you until you can support yourself. We will worry about that if that happens. But right now, mama, you are pregnant. This baby is here. Right now, they are safe.

It's okay to not feel brave. It doesn't mean you aren't. Every moment of taking a risk to do something that has horribly injured you in the past is brave and strong. Being strong doesn't mean not being scared. It means continuing on even when you are.

Take things one appointment at a time, one week at a time, one day at a time, or one moment at a time when you need to. Don't be afraid to soak in the joy of this pregnancy too. Don't be afraid to connect with your baby. Let yourself feel that when it happens. And don't be judgmental if you aren't connected. Sometimes being connected, having hope, and feeling the joy is just too scary.

Take care of yourself, mama. Feel your feelings. Distract when you need to. Lean on the people that support you in the ways that you need. Set boundaries to protect yourself when you need to. Ask for what you need at the time you need it - to be celebrated, to be understood, and to be cared for.

You can do this mama. You have already been through worse. You can endure this journey, fight this battle, and keep on going. You are strong enough.

I hope for you that one day soon you will be holding your living, breathing, crying baby in your arms. I want that for you more than anything. I want you to feel the relief, joy, and amazement of seeing your living, breathing baby outside of your body and of holding them on your chest and in your arms.

Pregnancy after loss is a long journey. Pregnancy after recurrent loss and fertility treatment is an even longer journey. But one day it will all be worth it. One day, as you hold your sleeping baby in a dark nursery in the middle of the night, writing a love letter to other loss moms, every shot, every medication, every ovulation stick, every tear shed, and every fear and worry that comes with pregnancy after loss will be worth the joy that this little one will bring into your life.

I am sending you all of my love, mama. You are not alone. Woman after woman has walked this path before you, beside you, and behind you. We are held together by an indescribably strong bond. We are all here for you. We are all here with you. We believe in your strength. You can do this.

Love always,

Kasey Schultz-Saindon

Mama to Lentil (11/18/2016), Danny (10/9/2017), and Ava.

"One day, as you hold your sleeping baby in a dark nursery in the middle of the night, writing a love letter to other loss moms, every shot, every medication, every ovulation stick, every tear shed, and every fear and worry that comes with pregnancy after loss will be worth the joy that this little one will bring into your life."

To the PAL Mama, With Love as Compass

Hey Mama.

I hope this letter finds you well, and you know how strong you are, right now, in this moment.
I want you to know something. I want you to know you are not alone. Not only are you not alone, you are seen. You are recognized. You, and all your babies, are beautiful, celebrated, and recognized.

As a queer woman, and as a mama to a starside child, I know what it's like to be unseen. To have those vital pieces of yourself hidden away, camouflaged under the surface of what the world sees. To correct and answer questions you don't feel like you should need to: is your husband excited, is this your first, aren't you thrilled. I would answer: my wife, no, I'm scared.

Pregnancy is a journey. How many times have we heard that, you and I? We know all too well it is perilous; one does not simply walk through pregnancy and birth. It is hard terrain, uncharted territory every time. You, warrior mama, journey as explorer and cartographer. The road isn't mapped until your feet have drawn it; there is no knowing where it ends until it disappears from underneath.

I've seen you, out on that terrifying terrain. I've seen you at work, at the store, at the holiday party. Maybe you haven't announced yet; there is no way to do that without remembering the one who couldn't stay. Maybe you have, and have already been barraged with platitudes and hopeful but worried hand pats. No one knew what to say after your heartbreak; no one is quite sure what to say now. Unless, that is, they have their own map tucked somewhere safe, tear stained with soft edges from being revisited so many times.

I recognize the one who carried life, who met with Death, and now walks heavier with the weight of loss. I see the pause before the smile, the one that doesn't quite reach your eyes, scared of the grief that hides in their depths. I know the hesitation in the hands that stray to your belly, guided by the promise of new life, slowed by the fear of new loss.

You, sweet mama, are a trailblazer. With love as your compass you navigate this world that so often overlooks you. Even if no one else does, you hold space for your little one; I know you wish you could be holding their hand as your body breathes with new life. You remember everything you ever knew about them. The days pass as you mark them: birth date, loss date, due date. You say their name; you whisper it to the shadows or scream it to the wind. I hear you.

While you are the only one who knows your journey, you are not alone. I know the sorrow, the unfairness of it all; I have served deep in the trenches of grief. I have waited for the sunrise after interminable nights, only for dawn to arrive steely gray and without warmth. I remember longing for the movements only I could feel; and when they finally came, I remember the panic that rushed in alongside the euphoria.

Brave mama, you are not alone.
When you voice the name of the one who couldn't stay, you are not alone.
When you aren't sure how to answer if this is your first

child, you are not alone.
When you awake in the night to count kicks, you are not alone.

You have a lifetime membership to a group no one wants to join. You are a loss mama; you have undertaken another arduous journey with no guarantee of a happy destination. Your strength is showing, mama.

You might not feel like you can enjoy this pregnancy as you did with another. The joys are tempered with worries, and every milestone casts a shadow. You know there's no safe zone, no week to reach that means the way forward is clear. Yet you rise each day and continue onward.

Your hopes and plans float in a sea of "ifs." The uncertainty itself is stressful, adding weight to your changing body. Still, you persist.

You hold a love that is precious, valid, and forever. You have made room in your heart to accommodate a child who could not stay in this world, and still expanded to introduce another.
Do you know how strong you are? I do.

And you take that love and let it guide you, let it light the unbroken trail ahead of you. And although you cannot see, out there in the darkness, that light shines for all of us who walk with you. We see you. We know you. We hold you and your babies up.

So, courageous mama, keep going; and know that you are not alone.

With love and light,

Marjanna Barber-Dubois

Mother to Oscar Prince, a starside wild child, and Lucy Danger, an earthside bright and shining light.

"I want you to know something. I want you to know you are not alone. Not only are you not alone, you are seen. You are recognized. You, and all your babies, are beautiful, celebrated, and recognized."

Dear Momma,

I know this is scary. The anxiety feels like it's gonna win. You're waiting for that next shoe to drop at any minute. It's hard to connect although you want to so badly. You want that innocence, that excitement back. That fear to be gone. The hope to be all consuming.

And I'm sorry. I'm sorry that that was taken from you, that your previous child or children were ripped away from you and you've been broken. But, I promise, the minute you hold this child in your arms, an all-consuming calmness will take over.

No, you won't be fully healed, and you may never be. But this baby changes you in a way you never thought possible. This baby will be a ray of sunshine on your darkest days. The most beautiful gift that their sibling(s) picked out for you.

And momma, you'll feel like you can breathe again. Oh friend, I pray that you'll see that. I pray that your heart will begin to mend. And I pray that you also always remember that you're never alone. You're a warrior. And so many of us are walking right alongside you crying out in prayer that soon enough, you too will be bringing home this child you so want to have and to hold.

Love, a momma to three here on earth and five up in heaven.

Amelia Kowalisyn

Founder of Emma's Footprints
Mother to Alex, Cameron, & Christian here on earth,
as well as Emma Rose and four additional sweet little
angels up in heaven.
https://www.facebook.com/EmmaKsfootprints/

"No, you won't be fully healed, and you may never be. But this baby changes you in a way you never thought possible. This baby will be a ray of sunshine on your darkest days."

To the Mother Pregnant After Child Loss

I too, have carried the weight of pregnancy and motherhood after the loss of one of my children. My own rainbow was placed in my arms, only 11 months after her brother's life had been taken from us as he slept.

She came barreling into our world after tragedy, leaving us no option but to face our grief and triggers. Her very presence in a place he'd been before her was a mountain for us to climb. She was living, her heart was beating, she was breathing, she was all of the things that had been stolen from us when he had suddenly died, and yet, she was every bit as much her own.

His death, and her life, have changed me in such important ways. I am a different mother this time around. A mother who straddles the line of mothering children who are still here, while mourning one who is not. A mother who has bent and broken, who bears the wounds of loss and trauma, but who is strong and resilient because of it. She was given a version of me that even I hadn't previously known, and every day of her existence teaches and nurtures that version of me more.

A rainbow baby does not make us whole again. They do not resolve our trauma or act as a replacement. They are not an end to the storm or a calming of the waves. Sometimes, most times, a rainbow appears before the storm is over.

As my husband and I age, every day will start and end

the same, with a piece of us missing. Our grief will never go away. It'll grow alongside our living children, just as the child we lost should have. We will have to continue to evolve in its different stages.

While we hope our rainbow babies never feel that their life is defined by the death of their sibling, they offer proof that amidst tragedy, joy can still be felt. They are a connection to the child we lost, a connection that continues to intricately weave the story of their sibling before them in a new way.

Yours will be too.

Jordan Peterson-DeRosier

Mama to Rowan, Sloan (12/4/16 - 7/3/17), Phoenix, & Valorie
@lifeofderosiers | lifeofderosiers.com

"His death, and her life, have changed me in such important ways. I am a different mother this time around. A mother who straddles the line of mothering children who are still here, while mourning one who is not. A mother who has bent and broken, who bears the wounds of loss and trauma, but who is strong and resilient because of it."

Dear Mama, Who is Terrified of Having to Say Goodbye Again

Are you scared?

Are you scared every day in this pregnancy that you will have to say goodbye again?

Say goodbye to your child, again?

Are you scared of not ever knowing how this will turn out? Of not knowing what the future holds? Of hearing those words, the silence, of breaking the news?

Is that fear suffocating you? Are you managing to fool everyone that you aren't consumed, crippled by that fear? Is it making it hard to breathe, to look forward, to relax into the moment, to bond and love your baby?

Just know this. You are not alone.

You are not alone. We are here. With you. This path of fear has been walked before, and is being walked with you, every day.

Please know this – fear does not have to win. Fear alone won't save your child. Nor will it hurt your child. It has no power over you. Fear comes in, uninvited. It does not have to stay.

To fight fear, is to embrace hope.

To fight fear, is to be enveloped in the light.

To fight fear, is to fall in love.

Dare to dream. Dare to fully fall in love with your child. Your baby. Your baby who is growing, moving and living every day. Growing, moving and living every day, because of you. Hold on to that thought today. Fall in love, in spite of that fear.

Embrace it. Embrace this time. Embrace the fear, and decide who is going to win.

I know how suffocating that fear is. How suffocating it can feel, when you are already struggling to breathe through the grief and the pain of already saying goodbye.

Sit with me for a while. Close your eyes, and just breathe.

Breathe in love, and breathe out fear.

Breathe in hope, and breathe out pain.

Breathe in and breathe out.

Ask yourself, what if I enjoyed this pregnancy to its fullest potential?

What if I silenced the thoughts? The fear that I might have to say goodbye?

What if I let myself fall in to a sea of love, and hope, and joy, and drown in the fleeting moment that this, this might all be okay?

Just lie here with me for a moment, and let's pretend together that fear isn't a part of this pregnancy.

You are not alone.

You are the strongest of warriors.

You are a survivor.

You are a wonderful mother.

You love, fiercely, with every cell of your body.

You are not alone.

Love, a mother also terrified of having to say goodbye again, pregnant after stillbirth.

Jessica Clasby-Monk

Mom to Leo Phoenix and Eli River
@thelegacyofleo

"Dare to dream. Dare to fully fall in love with your child. Your baby. Your baby who is growing, moving and living every day. Growing, moving and living every day, because of you. Hold on to that thought today. Fall in love, in spite of that fear.

Embrace it. Embrace this time. Embrace the fear, and decide who is going to win."

Beautiful Bearers of Life,

Wherever you are in your journey through pregnancy after loss, no matter what you are feeling or what thoughts race through your mind, I hope you find even the smallest bit of comfort in these final reminders:

You are not alone.

You, and your baby and your baby(ies) who died, are loved. So incredibly loved.

You are brave and courageous, walking side-by-side with uncertainty and fear.

Joy and hope can, and often do, exist with fear and doubt. All of the feelings are allowed.

You will get through this. One day, one moment, one breath at a time.

And we are here. Reaching out a hand in understanding and love, holding onto hope for and with you.

You are never, never alone.

About the Authors

Emily Long is the mama of two daughters, Grace and Lily both gone too soon, a grief + trauma counselor, human to two feisty cats, baker of bagels + bread, endless reader, lover of adventure, and occasional hermit. She is committed to supporting and advocating for families who experience the death of a child and writes frequently on the topic of pregnancy and infant loss. In her downtime, you can usually find her in her hermit house re-reading Harry Potter (yet again) or doing yoga (badly) at her favorite local yoga studio.

Lindsey Henke is the founder and Executive Director of Pregnancy After Loss Support, writer, clinical social worker, wife, and most importantly a mother to three beautiful children, a daughter and son who hold her hands and her eldest child, Nora, she holds in her heart. Lindsey's eldest daughter, Nora was stillborn after a healthy full-term pregnancy in December of 2012. Lindsey launched Pregnancy After Loss Support (PALS), a peer-to-peer support non-profit and online magazine that serves the mom who is navigating the difficult journey of a pregnancy that follows a previous loss in June of 2014, a few months after her second daughter, Zoe, was born healthy and alive.

Made in the USA
Coppell, TX
13 October 2023